Prayer to Mary Mother of God

Colouring Book with the Time-Honoured Prayer and 19 Florals

ESTHER PINCINI

Prayer to Mary Mother of God Colouring Book
with the Time-Honoured Prayer and 19 Florals
by Esther Pincini

Copyright © Magdalene Press 2018

ISBN 978-1-77335-113-1

No part of this publication may be reproduced, stored in a retrieval system,
or transmitted in any form or by any means, electronic, mechanical, photocopying,
recording or otherwise without written permission of the publisher.

Magdalene Press, 2018

Prayer to Mary Mother of God

To thee, O Mother of God,

Victorious leader of triumphant hosts,

We, thy servants,

Delivered from evil,

Sing our grateful thanks:

But since thou possessest invincible

Might, set us free from every calamity that we

May cry unto thee:

Hail, O Bride Unwedded.

Most glorious ever-virgin Mother of

Christ, our God,

Bring
our prayer
unto thy

Son and our God,

That by thee

He may save our souls.

All my hope I lay upon thee,

Divine Mother,

Preserve me

Beneath thy protection.

O Virgin Mother of God, despise

e not,
a sinner,

Who seek thy help and thy intercession;

For in thee hath my

Soul

hoped;

ave

mercy

upon me.

www.ingramcontent.com/pod-product-compliance
Lightning Source LLC
Chambersburg PA
CBHW051121110526
44589CB00026B/2995